Anyone who thinks heaven is not hot water behind a locked door has forgotten what it means to live.

—LUCY FRANK

HOME
SWEET
HOME

Created, published, and distributed by Knock Knock
6695 Green Valley Circle, #5167
Culver City, CA 90230
knockknockstuff.com
Knock Knock is a registered trademark of Knock Knock LLC

Printed in China

Illustrations by Kaitlin Brito

ISBN: 978-168349462-1
UPC: 825703503166

10 9 8 7 6 5 4 3 2 1

Cozy Hobbies YOU CAN DO in the bathroom

KNOCK KNOCK®
LOS ANGELES, CALIFORNIA

Your bathroom is your happy place . . . now make it your hobby place!

THE THRONE ROOM IS YOUR PRIVATE REFUGE & INNER SANCTUM, AND ONCE YOU'RE IN THERE WITH THE DOOR SHUT— preferably locked—you like to stay as long as possible, right? Basically forever? Of course you do! It's totally normal. You also enjoy learning new things and having fun. There's no reason you can't combine all these passions . . . and there are all kinds of reasons why you should!

Your bathroom is a haven for personal care and quietude, but it's also a secret creative incubator where you'll find easier access to your "flow" state, where time is suspended and things seem to come easily. Not toilet-related things, either . . . but art, new ideas, new skills, and FUN!

That's what this book is about: being in the bathroom—which is sometimes the only spot in the house for some "just me" time—while enjoying your leisure! This is the kind of extravagance our ancestors could only have dreamed of, and it's practically free! Why would you want to be anywhere but the bathroom?

Now go on and live your #bathlife!

TABLE OF CONTENTS

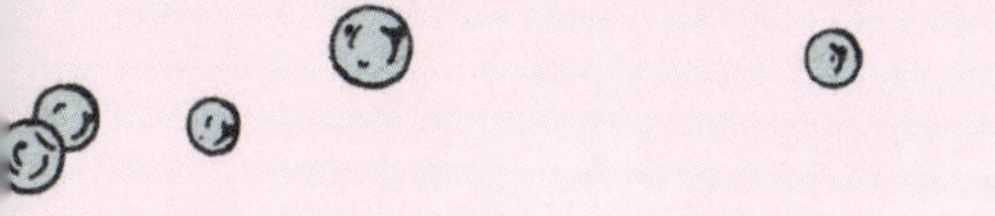

Felting

Make cozy woolen-ish fabric . . . in your cozy bathroom sink!

THE BASIC IDEA: Making felt is literally as easy as accidentally shrinking a sweater in the wash—minus the trauma and regret!

THE WHAT: You can make felt with stuff you probably already have on hand, or can get at the thrift store for super cheap. Felt can be made with all kinds of fibers, including old sweaters, scarves, and even fur clippings from your dog or cat. (It's not weird. Don't make it weird.) You don't even need real wool—rayon or synthetic fibers work, too!

THE WHY: Felting is an economical and eco-friendly way to recycle old woolen items, yarn, and fabrics. And then you can use it to make stuff: coin purses, coasters, tiny mushrooms, and little sweaters for your pet snake!

EXTRA CREDIT: If your felt is made from a natural fiber like wool, play around with DYEING it!

ALONE-TIME SCALE: About how long does this hobby take?

MAYBE LIKE 15 MINUTES? | AT LEAST THE LENGTH OF A MOVIE. OR THREE. | YOU COULD BE HERE FOREVER!

COZY HOBBY FYI'S

Do I need special tools?

○ Yes ○ No ⊗ It depends

How cheap is this hobby?

○ Free! ⊗ Cheap ○ Not cheap

Can I do this on the toilet?

○ Yes ○ Your call ⊗ At your own risk

Can I do this in a nice, warm bath?

○ Yes ⊗ Awkwardly, maybe? ○ A thousand times no

How many times will I have to leave the bathroom?

○ Never ever ⊗ Maybe once? ○ Ugh like 3 times

Witchcraft

Get all mystical & woo-woo—
in your magical loo-loo!

THE BASIC IDEA: Develop your casting & conjuring skills from the peace and privacy of your privy.

THE WHAT: Modern witchcraft is based on ancient practices, including herbal healing and earth-based goddess spirituality. It uses natural materials and esoteric forces to help you tap your intuitive wisdom and, hopefully, heal and nurture yourself—and the world!

THE WHY: Witchcraft is fun! It's groovy and grounding and mysterious and magical. Plus, it is uniquely suited to the throne room, as hobbies go, offering safety, convenience, and privacy for working with water, candles, and plants. And taking ritual baths is kind of a big deal in modern witchcraft.

EXTRA CREDIT: When guests see your bathroom, wave your hand dramatically and say, "This is where the magic happens."

ALONE-TIME SCALE: About how long does this hobby take?

MAYBE LIKE 15 MINUTES? | AT LEAST THE LENGTH OF A MOVIE. OR THREE. | YOU COULD BE HERE FOREVER!

COZY HOBBY FYI'S

Do I need special tools?

(X) Yes ( ) No ( ) It depends

How cheap is this hobby?

( ) Free! (X) Cheap ( ) Not cheap

Can I do this on the toilet?

( ) Yes ( ) Your call (X) At your own risk

Can I do this in a nice, warm bath?

(X) Yes ( ) Awkwardly, maybe? ( ) A thousand times no

How many times will I have to leave the bathroom?

(X) Never ever ( ) Maybe once? ( ) Ugh like 3 times

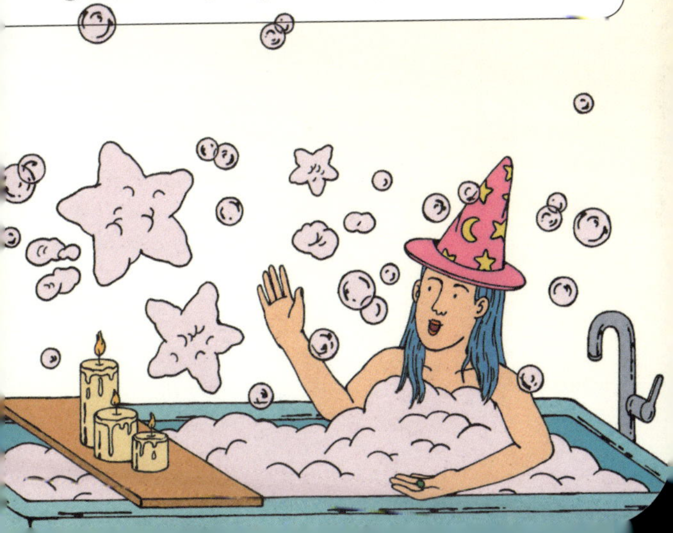

Volunteer!

Help make the world a better, kinder, healthier place . . . from your bathroom!

THE BASIC IDEA: You can support a cause dear to your heart, without getting off the toilet. What a time to be alive.

THE WHAT: Choose a nonprofit organization you believe in and would like to devote your time, talents, or money to. Lots of organizations need people to write letters or make cards for them, whether for children in the hospital, political prisoners, or others who are unjustly imprisoned.

THE WHY: Volunteering has been shown to help people feel happier in their lives and feel a deeper sense of purpose. Just because you want to be alone 90 percent of the time doesn't mean you can't make a contribution—in your own unique way!

ALONE-TIME SCALE: About how long does this hobby take?

MAYBE LIKE 15 MINUTES? — AT LEAST THE LENGTH OF A MOVIE. OR THREE. — YOU COULD BE HERE FOREVER!

COZY HOBBY FYI'S

Do I need special tools?
◯ Yes ⊗ No ◯ It depends

How cheap is this hobby?
⊗ Free! ◯ Cheap ◯ Not cheap

Can I do this on the toilet?
◯ Yes ⊗ Your call ◯ At your own risk

Can I do this in a nice, warm bath?
◯ Yes ◯ Awkwardly, maybe? ⊗ A thousand times no

How many times will I have to leave the bathroom?
⊗ Never ever ◯ Maybe once? ◯ Ugh like 3 times

EXTRA CREDIT: If you're feeling somewhat social, you can even make fundraising phone calls, charity phone trees, or do phone-banking for political candidates, parties, or causes! Who needs to know you're in the john?

Be an Influencer

Become a social media star without leaving the bathroom!

THE BASIC IDEA: Use the social media platform(s) of your choice to become a content creator!

THE WHAT: Turn your bathroom into a social media lab/studio! You can create a backdrop or use effects to hide the fact that you're in a bathroom . . . OR you can make your bathroom part of the show. After all, GRWM ("Get Ready with Me") videos are all the rage, and they're pretty much all shot in bathrooms!

THE WHY: Viewers, AKA people, are weirdly fascinated with looking at other people's private spaces, especially their bathrooms! This alone should guarantee you at least a handful of viewers.

EXTRA CREDIT: Make a whole channel about HOBBIES YOU CAN DO IN THE BATHROOM!

ALONE-TIME SCALE: About how long does this hobby take?

MAYBE LIKE 15 MINUTES? — AT LEAST THE LENGTH OF A MOVIE. OR THREE. — YOU COULD BE HERE FOREVER! (circled)

COZY HOBBY FYI'S

Do I need special tools?
(X) Yes ( ) No ( ) It depends

How cheap is this hobby?
( ) Free! ( ) Cheap (X) Not cheap

Can I do this on the toilet?
( ) Yes ( ) Your call (X) At your own risk

Can I do this in a nice, warm bath?
( ) Yes ( ) Awkwardly, maybe? (X) A thousand times no

How many times will I have to leave the bathroom?
( ) Never ever ( ) Maybe once? (X) Ugh like 3 times

There is no need to go to India or anywhere else to find peace. You will find that deep place of silence right in your room, your garden or even your bathtub.

—DR. ELISABETH KÜBLER-ROSS

Furniture Caning

Do you stan rattan?
Wrap your world in wicker!

THE BASIC IDEA: Give your décor a fresh-&-natural glowup. It's easier than you might think, especially if you work in the bathroom.

THE WHAT: Natural cane webbing is not only stylish, it's surprisingly durable. Use it on drawer fronts, picture frames, hurricane candle holders, etc.! All you really need is a staple gun and a big ol' tub of water to soak the webbing before you install it. Hmmm . . . now where might you find a tub of water?

THE WHY: Cane webbing is an easy way to update old furniture or cute-ify boring new furniture. IN THE BATHROOM!

HOT TIP: *Furniture caning is NOT hard, but there is a certain art to it. For that extra bit of confidence, watch YouTube DIY tutorials on how to do it.*

ALONE-TIME SCALE: About how long does this hobby take?

MAYBE LIKE 15 MINUTES? | AT LEAST THE LENGTH OF A MOVIE. OR THREE. | YOU COULD BE HERE FOREVER!

○ ○ ○ ○ ○ ○ (●) ○ ○ ○

COZY HOBBY FYI'S

Do I need special tools?

(X) Yes ○ No ○ It depends

How cheap is this hobby?

○ Free! ○ Cheap (X) Not cheap

Can I do this on the toilet?

○ Yes ○ Your call (X) At your own risk

Can I do this in a nice, warm bath?

○ Yes ○ Awkwardly, maybe? (X) A thousand times no

How many times will I have to leave the bathroom?

○ Never ever ○ Maybe once? (X) Ugh like 3 times

EXTRA CREDIT: Use your newfound caning prowess to give a boring piece of furniture (like an Ikea shelf) or cheap thrifted item a rich hippie makeover.

Brew Your Own Booze!

Make bathtub hooch like an old-time bootlegger!

THE BASIC IDEA: Brew your own beer or hard cider—in your bathroom!

THE WHAT: Making hooch isn't just for middle-aged dads and 1920s moonshiners! Depending on your equipment, you can do a lot of the work in the bathroom—including lots of cleaning and sanitizing of bottles and things. And since yeast likes to be warmish & darkish, a spare bathroom is great for fermenting!

THE WHY: Have you heard? YOU CAN MAKE YOUR OWN BOOZE. And it's not even illegal! Plus, homemade beer also has more nutrients than store-bought, but whatever.

HOT TIP: *This is definitely a hobby that will benefit from research: books, video tutorials, Reddit pages (you KNOW Reddit's full of homebrewing debates and wisdom).*

ALONE-TIME SCALE: About how long does this hobby take?

MAYBE LIKE 15 MINUTES? — AT LEAST THE LENGTH OF A MOVIE. OR THREE. — YOU COULD BE HERE FOREVER!

(Scale: 9 of 10 selected)

COZY HOBBY FYI'S

Do I need special tools?
(X) Yes ( ) No ( ) It depends

How cheap is this hobby?
( ) Free! ( ) Cheap (X) Not cheap

Can I do this on the toilet?
( ) Yes ( ) Your call (X) At your own risk

Can I do this in a nice, warm bath?
( ) Yes ( ) Awkwardly, maybe? (X) A thousand times no

How many times will I have to leave the bathroom?
( ) Never ever ( ) Maybe once? (X) Ugh like 3 times

EXTRA CREDIT: Try getting fancy with kombucha and even wine!

Candle Making

Get lit—literally—in the bathroom!

THE BASIC IDEA: You love candles, but you probably don't love how stupidly expensive they are. What's the DEAL with price of candles? Now you can free yourself from the tyranny of Big Candle, because you're going to make your own.

THE WHAT: Make candles with the wax of your choice or recycle leftover wax from old candles. Tapers, votives, birthday & holiday candles! Candles in jars! Candles candles CANDLES . . . in your bathroom bathroom BATHROOM! You can even reuse the jars, glasses, or tins your old candles came in. Be careful—melted wax gets hot!

THE WHY: Candle-making is economical, creative, fun, and pleasantly challenging. Once you get the hang of it, you can start giving them as gifts and save even more money!

ALONE-TIME SCALE: About how long does this hobby take?

MAYBE LIKE 15 MINUTES? | AT LEAST THE LENGTH OF A MOVIE. OR THREE. | YOU COULD BE HERE FOREVER!

(Rating: 2 of 10)

COZY HOBBY FYI'S

Do I need special tools?
(X) Yes ( ) No ( ) It depends

How cheap is this hobby?
( ) Free! (X) Cheap ( ) Not cheap

Can I do this on the toilet?
( ) Yes ( ) Your call (X) At your own risk

Can I do this in a nice, warm bath?
( ) Yes ( ) Awkwardly, maybe? (X) A thousand times no

How many times will I have to leave the bathroom?
( ) Never ever (X) Maybe once? ( ) Ugh like 3 times

HOT TIP: *You can purchase wicks in bulk (as well as wax) online and use a plug-in wax melter. Hang your tapers on a towel rack as they solidify.*

EXTRA CREDIT: Make scented candles and make your own wicks from untreated cotton!

POWDER ROOM NUGGETS!

DID YOU KNOW?

About 80 percent of men and 69 percent of women use their phone on the toilet, according to a 2018 study. The study also showed that 96 percent of Americans under the age of 23 won't go to the bathroom without their phone. Somehow, this isn't a huge surprise.

Laminate Stuff!

Seriously: Is there anything a laminator can't *do?!*

THE BASIC IDEA: Laminate everything you've ever wanted to laminate . . . in the loo!

THE WHAT: In olden days, laminators were big & expensive, and only copy shop employees knew the intoxicating power of lamination. No longer! Now you too can preserve important papers in sturdy clear plastic: ID cards, photos, recipe cards, ticket stubs, and other mementos. Laminate dried flowers. Laminate your life!

THE WHY: It's oddly satisfying to encase precious items in clear plastic, keeping them protected and safe. Once you start, you'll never want to stop. Can you feel the excitement? Just don't electrocute yourself.

EXTRA CREDIT: Make gifts: bookmarks, photo magnets, and weird earrings, just for starters!

ALONE-TIME SCALE: About how long does this hobby take?

MAYBE LIKE 15 MINUTES? (circled) — AT LEAST THE LENGTH OF A MOVIE. OR THREE. — YOU COULD BE HERE FOREVER!

COZY HOBBY FYI'S

Do I need special tools?
(X) Yes ( ) No ( ) It depends

How cheap is this hobby?
( ) Free! ( ) Cheap (X) Not cheap

Can I do this on the toilet?
( ) Yes ( ) Your call (X) At your own risk

Can I do this in a nice, warm bath?
( ) Yes ( ) Awkwardly, maybe? (X) A thousand times no

How many times will I have to leave the bathroom?
(X) Never ever ( ) Maybe once? ( ) Ugh like 3 times

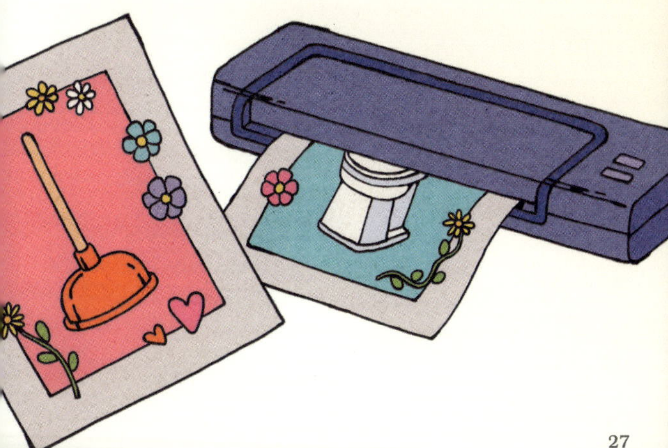

Flower Arranging

Spruce up your space with floral artwork—from the john!

THE BASIC IDEA: Create lovely bouquets for yourself and others. FROM YOUR BATHROOM. That's right—you can turn your throne room into a floral studio. No one has to know.

THE WHAT: Connect with the beauty of nature—and your own creative instincts—while freshening up your nest at the same time. Place bouquets on your nightstand, desk, kitchen sink, or the back of your toilet. (Doesn't your toilet deserve some flowers? It works so hard!)

THE WHY: Flower arranging is super soothing, and giving flowers to others feels so good. Homemade bouquets are especially meaningful (which is convenient, since they're also much cheaper)!

ALONE-TIME SCALE: About how long does this hobby take?

MAYBE LIKE 15 MINUTES? — AT LEAST THE LENGTH OF A MOVIE. OR THREE. — YOU COULD BE HERE FOREVER!

(Selected: 1 of 10)

COZY HOBBY FYI'S

Do I need special tools?
○ Yes ○ No ⊗ It depends

How cheap is this hobby?
○ Free! ⊗ Cheap ○ Not cheap

Can I do this on the toilet?
○ Yes ○ Your call ⊗ At your own risk

Can I do this in a nice, warm bath?
○ Yes ⊗ Awkwardly, maybe? ○ A thousand times no

How many times will I have to leave the bathroom?
⊗ Never ever ○ Maybe once? ○ Ugh like 3 times

EXTRA CREDIT: If you're short on blooms, get artsy and experimental with herbs, vegetable greens, houseplant cuttings, wildflowers, and even weeds, if they're cute!

Strength Training

Pump iron. Shower. Repeat!

THE BASIC IDEA: Get ripped, shredded, grated—or whatever the kids are calling it these days—from the cozy comfort of your comfy-cozy bathroom.

THE WHAT: Using hand weights (or other heavy-ish objects), you can totally build your muscles without even standing up, much less leaving the house! TONS of strength-training moves are performed lying or sitting down, like chest flyes, glute bridges, Russian twists, scissor kicks, skullcrushers, and garlic presses. (OK that one's made-up.)

THE WHY: Consider the time and money you'll save not going to the gym. It fairly boggles the mind! Bonus: No one else's sweat & germs. No other people, period! Working out in the john saves wear-and-tear on your joints! Plus, you'll avoid the danger of tripping over barbells. (It happens!)

ALONE-TIME SCALE: About how long does this hobby take?

MAYBE LIKE 15 MINUTES? — AT LEAST THE LENGTH OF A MOVIE. OR THREE. — YOU COULD BE HERE FOREVER!

COZY HOBBY FYI'S

Do I need special tools?
(X) Yes ◯ No ◯ It depends

How cheap is this hobby?
◯ Free! ◯ Cheap (X) Not cheap

Can I do this on the toilet?
◯ Yes (X) Your call ◯ At your own risk

Can I do this in a nice, warm bath?
◯ Yes (X) Awkwardly, maybe? ◯ A thousand times no

How many times will I have to leave the bathroom?
(X) Never ever ◯ Maybe once? ◯ Ugh like 3 times

HOT TIP: *Watch videos on how to engage your core and use proper form—it can make all the difference in getting ripped or getting injured.*

EXTRA CREDIT: Once you're done getting pumped up, do a whole session of stretching—sitting in the bath!

Soap Carving

Make clean art . . . in your washroom!

THE BASIC IDEA: Learn how to make your own carved sculptures with a simple bar of soap and plastic knife!

THE WHAT: Carve a little bird. Make whatever you can dream up. Get super meta and sculpt something "dirty," like . . . a toilet!

THE WHY: There's a reason soap carving is often taught to kids. Soap is an accessible, unintimidating medium for learning how to carve, especially compared to stone or wood. Plus, it's cheap. It's soap! Just don't eat it.

EXTRA CREDIT: You can also carve a design into the flat side of a bar of soap, then coat that with in ink or paint to create block print art. Decorate wrapping paper or your walls!

ALONE-TIME SCALE: About how long does this hobby take?

MAYBE LIKE 15 MINUTES? — AT LEAST THE LENGTH OF A MOVIE. OR THREE. — YOU COULD BE HERE FOREVER!

COZY HOBBY FYI'S

Do I need special tools?
◯ Yes ◯ No ⊗ It depends

How cheap is this hobby?
◯ Free! ⊗ Cheap ◯ Not cheap

Can I do this on the toilet?
⊗ Yes ◯ Your call ◯ At your own risk

Can I do this in a nice, warm bath?
◯ Yes ⊗ Awkwardly, maybe? ◯ A thousand times no

How many times will I have to leave the bathroom?
⊗ Never ever ◯ Maybe once? ◯ Ugh like 3 times

POTTY *talk*

As a kid, I'd go into the bathroom when I was having a tantrum. I'd be in the bathroom crying, studying myself in the mirror. I was preparing for future roles.

—ADAM SANDLER

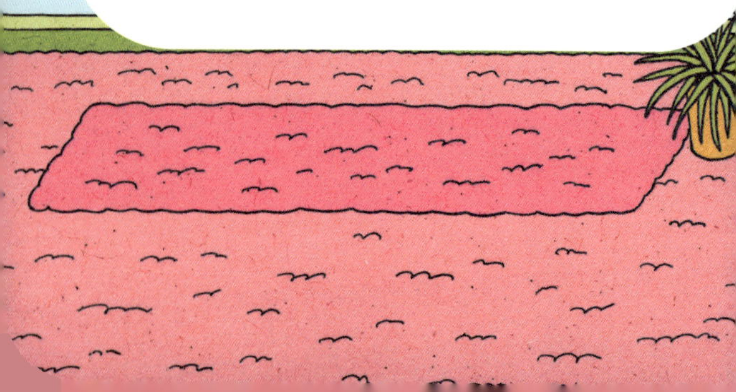

Calligraphy

Write letters like a fancy person in olden tymes!

THE BASIC IDEA: Calligraphy is beautiful hand-lettering that can be created with a pen or paintbrush, or by using special calligraphy markers & such.

THE WHAT: You can teach yourself calligraphy by following one of many tutorials online. Pick a style you'd like to learn and begin with the alphabet. Don't be hard on yourself if it looks less-than-pro. Calligraphy is kind of like pizza—even when it's not very good, it's awesome.

THE WHY: Calligraphy is so beautiful, when people see elegant curlicues coming out of your pen, they'll think you're either a magical being or really cool robot. Win-win. Calligraphy jazzes up envelopes, greeting cards, gifts, labels, etc.! Who knows—if you get good, you could even do it for extra income! Some people pay good money to have swirly letters on their wedding invites!

ALONE-TIME SCALE: About how long does this hobby take?

MAYBE LIKE 15 MINUTES? — AT LEAST THE LENGTH OF A MOVIE. OR THREE. — YOU COULD BE HERE FOREVER!

COZY HOBBY FYI'S

Do I need special tools?
(X) Yes ○ No ○ It depends

How cheap is this hobby?
○ Free! ○ Cheap (X) Not cheap

Can I do this on the toilet?
(X) Yes ○ Your call ○ At your own risk

Can I do this in a nice, warm bath?
○ Yes ○ Awkwardly, maybe? (X) A thousand times no

How many times will I have to leave the bathroom?
○ Never ever (X) Maybe once? ○ Ugh like 3 times

HOT TIP: *Use a calligraphy marker, which comes equipped with a special wide/flat nib that makes all those seemingly 3-dimensional, ribbon-like curves so much easier!*

EXTRA CREDIT: Learn calligraphy from another part of the world!

Stretching

Relax and let loose—literally!

THE BASIC IDEA: Stretch your body and soothe your spirit in the comfy-coziness of your powder room!

THE WHAT: Stretch tight muscles—and gently loosen all the other stuff, too! It's weird to think about, but stretching your muscles also means stretching your nerves, blood vessels, skin, tendons, ligaments, joints, and lymphatic system. A warm bath can be a good moment for gentle stretching, or after a shower, when the bathroom is steamed-up and your muscles are warm. Just be safe, dude!

THE WHY: Stretching is so, so good for you—it improves muscle performance, balance, circulation, sleep, and even can release endorphins. Plus, it's free!

EXTRA CREDIT: Try to stretch for ten minutes, at least 3–4 times a week. Make up your own names for your stretches (e.g., Grumpy Snake, Banana Split, etc.)!

ALONE-TIME SCALE: About how long does this hobby take?

MAYBE LIKE 15 MINUTES? | AT LEAST THE LENGTH OF A MOVIE. OR THREE. | YOU COULD BE HERE FOREVER!

(X) 1 ( ) 2 ( ) 3 ( ) 4 ( ) 5 ( ) 6 ( ) 7 ( ) 8 ( ) 9 ( ) 10

COZY HOBBY FYI'S

Do I need special tools?

( ) Yes (X) No ( ) It depends

How cheap is this hobby?

(X) Free! ( ) Cheap ( ) Not cheap

Can I do this on the toilet?

( ) Yes (X) Your call ( ) At your own risk

Can I do this in a nice, warm bath?

(X) Yes ( ) Awkwardly, maybe? ( ) A thousand times no

How many times will I have to leave the bathroom?

(X) Never ever ( ) Maybe once? ( ) Ugh like 3 times

Cutting Hair!

You can do this.
Stop paying other people!

THE BASIC IDEA: Learn to cut hair, including your own! It is possible. You can do this!

THE WHAT: The internet has destroyed so many things—personal privacy, record stores, the fabric of society . . . but it's also given us the ability to cut our own hair with confidence. So, there's that?

THE WHY: Haircuts are expensive! If your hair grows fast, you probably need a trim at least once a month. But you can extend the life of your salon cuts—or quit the salon altogether—with a pair of scissors and some how-to videos.

EXTRA CREDIT: If you want total liberation from the salon, check out amazing & ingenious DIY hair-do videos. You too can master the effortlessly undone one-minute French twist!

ALONE-TIME SCALE: About how long does this hobby take?

MAYBE LIKE 15 MINUTES? — AT LEAST THE LENGTH OF A MOVIE. OR THREE. — YOU COULD BE HERE FOREVER!

COZY HOBBY FYI'S

Do I need special tools?

◯ Yes ◯ No ⊗ It depends

How cheap is this hobby?

⊗ Free! ◯ Cheap ◯ Not cheap

Can I do this on the toilet?

◯ Yes ◯ Your call ⊗ At your own risk

Can I do this in a nice, warm bath?

◯ Yes ⊗ Awkwardly, maybe? ◯ A thousand times no

How many times will I have to leave the bathroom?

⊗ Never ever ◯ Maybe once? ◯ Ugh like 3 times

POWDER ROOM NUGGETS!

DID YOU KNOW?

According to a 2022 survey, over half of Americans hide out in the bathroom looking for peace & quiet. The number shoots to 62 percent for people with kids. British men spend an average of seven hours per year in the loo seeking refuge from their families, according to a 2018 poll. About 25 percent said that without these visits to their safe place, they "don't know how they'd cope." Confirmation: It's not just you.

Make Your Own Paper!

It's crafting, recycling, and art-making at the same time—in the can!

THE BASIC IDEA: Turn your junk mail, paper bags, newspapers, scrap paper, etc., into soulful, textural handcrafted paper.

THE WHAT: With paper, water, a blender, and a piece of screen, you can make paper! Like, cool arty paper!

THE WHY: Making paper is kind of like making cookies . . . the ingredients are so cheap and simple, and yet, somehow, the end is much more than the sum of its parts. It's the kind of process that makes you feel like you're part of something super ancient and borderline magic. Plus, it's actually useful. And quite pretty!

ALONE-TIME SCALE: About how long does this hobby take?

MAYBE LIKE 15 MINUTES? — AT LEAST THE LENGTH OF A MOVIE. OR THREE. — YOU COULD BE HERE FOREVER!

(4 of 10 selected)

COZY HOBBY FYI'S

Do I need special tools?
(X) Yes ( ) No ( ) It depends

How cheap is this hobby?
( ) Free! (X) Cheap ( ) Not cheap

Can I do this on the toilet?
( ) Yes ( ) Your call (X) At your own risk

Can I do this in a nice, warm bath?
( ) Yes ( ) Awkwardly, maybe? (X) A thousand times no

How many times will I have to leave the bathroom?
( ) Never ever (X) Maybe once? ( ) Ugh like 3 times

HOT TIP: *Once you've made paper, you can do other things with it. Write a special note to someone! Use it for wrapping gifts! Make a picture! Make a little paper lantern! Make jewelry!*

EXTRA CREDIT: Use food coloring to make colorful paper. Or get really fancy and learn to make paper from rags, which is totally a doable thing!

Make a Vision Board!

Create a vision for your dream life . . . in the can! (Yes, you can!)

THE BASIC IDEA: Make an inspiring collage of images that represent your life goals. It couldn't hurt, and it just might work.

THE WHAT: Gather pics of things you want in your life—or that spark feelings you'd like to feel. Gaze at it daily. If all goes as planned, your life will start to resemble your collage! How, you ask? Is it the "law of attraction"? Magic? Um, maybe! At the very least, it's a fun way to spend alone time in the loo.

THE WHY: Besides they're cheap, fun & maybe magical? Visualization has been proven to help athletes perform better—it's science! Plus, what harm could it do? Just don't use a picture of a magic portal to a land of giant flesh-eating plants.

ALONE-TIME SCALE: About how long does this hobby take?

MAYBE LIKE 15 MINUTES? | AT LEAST THE LENGTH OF A MOVIE. OR THREE. | YOU COULD BE HERE FOREVER!

COZY HOBBY FYI'S

Do I need special tools?
(X) Yes ( ) No ( ) It depends

How cheap is this hobby?
(X) Free! ( ) Cheap ( ) Not cheap

Can I do this on the toilet?
(X) Yes ( ) Your call ( ) At your own risk

Can I do this in a nice, warm bath?
( ) Yes ( ) Awkwardly, maybe? (X) A thousand times no

How many times will I have to leave the bathroom?
( ) Never ever (X) Maybe once? ( ) Ugh like 3 times

EXTRA CREDIT: Make vision boards for different parts of your life. You might make one for romance and one for your health and a general one for your general daily life. There are no rules of how many you can create. It's a more the merrier type of thing.

Gardening

Care for plants in the comfort of your comfort station!

THE BASIC IDEA: Grow plants and nurture them without ever leaving the john!

THE WHAT: Your bathroom is a nursery waiting to happen, 'cause if there's one room in any house that plants love, it's the bathroom. Why? Most houseplants come from the tropics & like high humidity and filtered light. Plus, it's the most convenient place to work with dirt and water.

THE WHY: Plants improve the air by filtering airborne toxins and even reducing dust! Plus, most tropical plants can be easily propagated, which means you can make lots of plants from one plant . . . for free.

EXTRA CREDIT: Bring your plants to the sink and give their leaves a good rinsing-off (those things get dusty!), and let the water run out the bottom of the pots to help remove any built-up salt from the soil.

ALONE-TIME SCALE: About how long does this hobby take?

MAYBE LIKE 15 MINUTES? — AT LEAST THE LENGTH OF A MOVIE. OR THREE. — YOU COULD BE HERE FOREVER!

COZY HOBBY FYI'S

Do I need special tools?

○ Yes ○ No ⊗ It depends

How cheap is this hobby?

○ Free! ○ Cheap ⊗ Not cheap

Can I do this on the toilet?

○ Yes ○ Your call ⊗ At your own risk

Can I do this in a nice, warm bath?

○ Yes ○ Awkwardly, maybe? ⊗ A thousand times no

How many times will I have to leave the bathroom?

○ Never ever ○ Maybe once? ⊗ Ugh like 3 times

Make an Album! Like, a Record!

Become a real recording artist—without leaving your bathroom.

THE BASIC IDEA: Create your own music and record it in your own private studio—aka bathtub/shower!

THE WHAT: Recording music at home is a tried-and-true approach, from Julie London (1960's *Julie . . . At Home*) to Billie Eilish (2019's *When We All Fall Asleep, Where Do We Go?*). Guess what part of your house has the best musical acoustics . . . Yep, the bathroom! Young Lennon & McCartney started out playing in the empty bathtub at John's mum's house. If it's good enough for them . . .

THE WHY: Home recording is easier and more affordable than it's ever been, thanks to digital technology, but analog setups are still very doable, even in a small space. Plus, maybe you'll go viral!

ALONE-TIME SCALE: About how long does this hobby take?

MAYBE LIKE 15 MINUTES? | AT LEAST THE LENGTH OF A MOVIE. OR THREE. | YOU COULD BE HERE FOREVER!

(Scale of 10; the 10th position, YOU COULD BE HERE FOREVER!, is circled)

COZY HOBBY FYI'S

Do I need special tools?

(X) Yes ( ) No ( ) It depends

How cheap is this hobby?

( ) Free! ( ) Cheap (X) Not cheap

Can I do this on the toilet?

( ) Yes ( ) Your call (X) At your own risk

Can I do this in a nice, warm bath?

( ) Yes ( ) Awkwardly, maybe? (X) A thousand times no

How many times will I have to leave the bathroom?

( ) Never ever ( ) Maybe once? (X) Ugh like 3 times

EXTRA CREDIT: Make your masterpiece super hip and meta! Record a concept album about recording a concept album in your bathroom. Include references to other artists who have recorded albums at home, like MGMT and Bon Iver. Then do a podcast about the making of the album!

POTTY *talk*

If you feel overwhelmed . . . escape to your bathroom. Just take some breaths in. Exhale. Do that about ten times.

—ALICIA KEYS

Aromatherapy

Turn your bathroom into an olfactory pleasure dome!

THE BASIC IDEA: Enchant your nose and nurture your spirit with the power of natural essential oils.

THE WHAT: Essential oils are derived from trees, plants, and fruit of all kinds. Different scents are believed to have unique effects on us: lavender for calming, lemon for waking up, eucalyptus for congestion, and so forth. Add them to a diffuser or wax melter, sprinkle them in your bath or on a candle, or make your own room spray! Doesn't your bathroom deserve to smell wonderful?

THE WHY: Aromatherapy is fun, and in some cases, backed by science. For example, lavender is proven to help reduce anxiety and depressive symptoms. Plus, smells that have positive associations can help boost your mood. Just ask a realtor about making cinnamon rolls and apple pie!

ALONE-TIME SCALE: About how long does this hobby take?

MAYBE LIKE 15 MINUTES? | AT LEAST THE LENGTH OF A MOVIE. OR THREE. | YOU COULD BE HERE FOREVER!

COZY HOBBY FYI'S

Do I need special tools?
(X) Yes ◯ No ◯ It depends

How cheap is this hobby?
◯ Free! (X) Cheap ◯ Not cheap

Can I do this on the toilet?
◯ Yes (X) Your call ◯ At your own risk

Can I do this in a nice, warm bath?
(X) Yes ◯ Awkwardly, maybe? ◯ A thousand times no

How many times will I have to leave the bathroom?
◯ Never ever (X) Maybe once? ◯ Ugh like 3 times

EXTRA CREDIT: Mix your favorite scents together and invent your own mind-soothing, mood-boosting scented cocktail.

Balloon Animals

Become the least-boring grownup in all the land (or on the block).

THE BASIC IDEA: Mesmerize kids and kids-at-heart with your godlike ability to create life from rubber!

THE WHAT: For too long, clowns have lorded their powers of creation over the rest of us. No more! The secret knowledge of making inflatable wiener dogs is for all the people. Just start simple, and give yourself a head start by using those long-and-skinny balloons made special for the job!

THE WHY: It's cheap, satisfying & great for parties. You could even make it a side-hustle!

HOT TIP: *The library has step-by-step guides & YouTube is a wonderland of how-to-make-balloon-animal videos. The whole world wants you to make balloon animals!*

EXTRA CREDIT: Make hats and cutlasses for a whole army of young buccaneers.

ALONE-TIME SCALE: About how long does this hobby take?

MAYBE LIKE 15 MINUTES? | AT LEAST THE LENGTH OF A MOVIE. OR THREE. | YOU COULD BE HERE FOREVER!

COZY HOBBY FYI'S

Do I need special tools?
(X) Yes ( ) No ( ) It depends

How cheap is this hobby?
( ) Free! (X) Cheap ( ) Not cheap

Can I do this on the toilet?
(X) Yes ( ) Your call ( ) At your own risk

Can I do this in a nice, warm bath?
(X) Yes ( ) Awkwardly, maybe? ( ) A thousand times no

How many times will I have to leave the bathroom?
( ) Never ever (X) Maybe once? ( ) Ugh like 3 times

Paint-by-Numbers!

If you can match a number to a tub of paint, you can be a masterful artiste!

THE BASIC IDEA: Get a paint-by-numbers kit, don a beret, and create beautiful paintings FROM THE BATHROOM!

THE WHAT: Painting-by-numbers is fun, simple, and affordable. Each kit comes with a pre-printed canvas, paint, and at least one kinda crappy brush. All you need is a glass of water and paper towels (for brush cleaning).

THE WHY: Who doesn't need gorgeous artwork to gaze upon, either from the toilet, or anywhere else in your home? Imagine guests looking around your space. Suddenly, their jaws drop. After recovering from their shock and wonderment they ask, "Who made all these incredible paintings?" You glance away with a sly half-smile, then look them straight in the eye and proclaim, "I did. In the bathroom."

ALONE-TIME SCALE: About how long does this hobby take?

MAYBE LIKE 15 MINUTES? — AT LEAST THE LENGTH OF A MOVIE. OR THREE. — YOU COULD BE HERE FOREVER!

COZY HOBBY FYI'S

Do I need special tools?
(X) Yes ( ) No ( ) It depends

How cheap is this hobby?
( ) Free! ( ) Cheap (X) Not cheap

Can I do this on the toilet?
(X) Yes ( ) Your call ( ) At your own risk

Can I do this in a nice, warm bath?
( ) Yes ( ) Awkwardly, maybe? (X) A thousand times no

How many times will I have to leave the bathroom?
( ) Never ever (X) Maybe once? ( ) Ugh like 3 times

EXTRA CREDIT: Actually frame your paintings and hang them up. Or sell 'em on Etsy so other folks can marvel at your craft from the comfort of their own can!

Self-Esteem Mirror Work

You are beautiful. You are capable. You are worth it!

THE BASIC IDEA: Use your bathroom mirror as a tool to rebuild your self-esteem and heal your inner child (really!).

THE WHAT: Gaze into your very own windows-to-the-soul (your eyes!), and give yourself heartfelt compliments. You might feel silly, but give it time to work its magic.

THE WHY: There's something truly alchemical about this mirror-talk trick. We all need emotional and mental boosts, and there's no one better to give that to you than . . . well, YOU.

HOT TIP: *The trick is to maintain strong eye contact with yourself and repeat your affirmations as many times as you need. Here's one to get you started: I AM CAPABLE OF BEING THE PERSON I WANT TO BE.*

ALONE-TIME SCALE: About how long does this hobby take?

MAYBE LIKE 15 MINUTES? | AT LEAST THE LENGTH OF A MOVIE. OR THREE. | YOU COULD BE HERE FOREVER!

COZY HOBBY FYI'S

Do I need special tools?
○ Yes ⊗ No ○ It depends

How cheap is this hobby?
⊗ Free! ○ Cheap ○ Not cheap

Can I do this on the toilet?
○ Yes ⊗ Your call ○ At your own risk

Can I do this in a nice, warm bath?
⊗ Yes ○ Awkwardly, maybe? ○ A thousand times no

How many times will I have to leave the bathroom?
⊗ Never ever ○ Maybe once? ○ Ugh like 3 times

EXTRA CREDIT: Write your affirmations on sticky notes and stick 'em to your mirror. Every time you use the bathroom, do a rep of at three affirmations. It's like a workout for your mental health.

POWDER ROOM NUGGETS!

DID YOU KNOW?

Every year about 235,000 Americans over age 15 visit the emergency room because of injuries suffered in the bathroom. The most dangerous activities are bathing, showering, and getting out of the tub or shower. Emphasis on *getting out*: only 2.2 percent of injuries occur while getting *into* the tub or shower, but 9.8 percent occur while getting *out*!

Tie-Dyeing

Make trippy shirts, skirts, bandanas, dog onesies . . . in the bathtub!

THE BASIC IDEA: Using humble rubber bands and fabric dye, you can enliven boring white fabric with fanciful colors and eye-catching designs . . . in your bathtub or sink!

THE WHAT: Much like hippies' favorite smokable herb, tie-dye has come SUCH A LONG WAY since the 1960s. Heck, it's come a long way since the 1990s! Fabric dye today is much more vibrant and easy-to-use. You can even get handy tie-dye kits with everything you need.

THE WHY: People literally pay money for boho fabrics . . . what cheaper way to refresh your throw pillows, curtains, t-shirts . . . or design your next festival lewk!

EXTRA CREDIT: Try one of those incredibly complicated designs usually seen on professionally-dyed Grateful Dead shirts.

ALONE-TIME SCALE: About how long does this hobby take?

MAYBE LIKE 15 MINUTES? — AT LEAST THE LENGTH OF A MOVIE. OR THREE. — YOU COULD BE HERE FOREVER!

(Circled: 4 of 10)

COZY HOBBY FYI'S

Do I need special tools?
(X) Yes ( ) No ( ) It depends

How cheap is this hobby?
( ) Free! (X) Cheap ( ) Not cheap

Can I do this on the toilet?
( ) Yes ( ) Your call (X) At your own risk

Can I do this in a nice, warm bath?
( ) Yes ( ) Awkwardly, maybe? (X) A thousand times no

How many times will I have to leave the bathroom?
( ) Never ever ( ) Maybe once? (X) Ugh like 3 times

Prepare for the Zombie (or Other) Apocalypse!

Get stocked and prepped for all possible scenarios . . . then take a nice bath!

THE BASIC IDEA: Prepare for unlikely-but-possible situations, from earthquakes to floods to dystopian robots.

THE WHAT: Getting prepared isn't just a hobby for kooky survivalist types. It's really for all of us, since simply being alive involves a degree of risk. Learn about your specific area and consult local authorities for guidance on preparedness. The Red Cross or government websites are good starting points.

THE WHY: Most people feel like they don't have time to worry about disaster preparedness. It's overwhelming! That's

ALONE-TIME SCALE: About how long does this hobby take?

MAYBE LIKE 15 MINUTES? | AT LEAST THE LENGTH OF A MOVIE. OR THREE. | YOU COULD BE HERE FOREVER!

COZY HOBBY FYI'S

Do I need special tools?
(X) Yes ( ) No ( ) It depends

How cheap is this hobby?
( ) Free! ( ) Cheap (X) Not cheap

Can I do this on the toilet?
( ) Yes (X) Your call ( ) At your own risk

Can I do this in a nice, warm bath?
( ) Yes ( ) Awkwardly, maybe? (X) A thousand times no

How many times will I have to leave the bathroom?
( ) Never ever ( ) Maybe once? (X) Ugh like 3 times

why you should think of this as a HOBBY—something you do a little at a time, for amusement—or to procrastinate on work! Over time, you'll find yourself becoming more and more prepared. And that sense of security is almost as nice as a hot bath. (Do that, too.)

EXTRA CREDIT: Make a calendar to remember when to rotate & replace soon-to-expire items (like batteries, zombie repellant, etc.).

Learn to Cast Rune Stones

Read fortunes like a Viking!

THE BASIC IDEA: Rune stones are used for divination and fortune-telling—kinda like Tarot cards, but with an earthy Norse twist!

THE WHAT: Runes are small objects inscribed with ancient Norse symbols, used for intuitive & cosmic guidance. For maximum soothsaying power, make your own runes from something natural like wood, rocks, or clay. Air-dry clay = EVEN LESS WORK.

THE WHY: Get ancient cosmic clarity, groove on the Tolkienesque vibes, and predict your whole future from the potty! Plus, you don't have to be even remotely Scandinavian!

HOT TIP: *YouTube is an excellent beginner-friendly resource for learning how to make rune stones, what the symbols mean, and how to use them.*

ALONE-TIME SCALE: About how long does this hobby take?

MAYBE LIKE 15 MINUTES? | AT LEAST THE LENGTH OF A MOVIE. OR THREE. | YOU COULD BE HERE FOREVER!

COZY HOBBY FYI'S

Do I need special tools?
(X) Yes ( ) No ( ) It depends

How cheap is this hobby?
( ) Free! (X) Cheap ( ) Not cheap

Can I do this on the toilet?
( ) Yes ( ) Your call (X) At your own risk

Can I do this in a nice, warm bath?
( ) Yes (X) Awkwardly, maybe? ( ) A thousand times no

How many times will I have to leave the bathroom?
(X) Never ever ( ) Maybe once? ( ) Ugh like 3 times

Daydreaming

Almost everything you have or are now, started as a thought or a daydream of some sort.

THE BASIC IDEA: Spend some of your quality bathroom time dreaming up new plans and discovering new desires, all the while making your hair shinier or scrubbing the tub.

THE WHAT: Studies show that the reason we have so many good ideas in the shower is because our minds go on autopilot. While you're following your long-established shower routine, your mind is free to open itself up to wander and yes, even daydream.

THE WHY: Daydreaming has been shown to reduce stress, be a positive way to manage anxiety and it also helps with solving problems and can help you with self-discovery and creativity. There is no downside to thinking just to think, dreaming just to dream.

ALONE-TIME SCALE: About how long does this hobby take?

MAYBE LIKE 15 MINUTES? — AT LEAST THE LENGTH OF A MOVIE. OR THREE. — YOU COULD BE HERE FOREVER!

COZY HOBBY FYI'S

Do I need special tools?
○ Yes ⊗ No ○ It depends

How cheap is this hobby?
⊗ Free! ○ Cheap ○ Not cheap

Can I do this on the toilet?
⊗ Yes ○ Your call ○ At your own risk

Can I do this in a nice, warm bath?
⊗ Yes ○ Awkwardly, maybe? ○ A thousand times no

How many times will I have to leave the bathroom?
⊗ Never ever ○ Maybe once? ○ Ugh like 3 times

HOT TIP: *Don't judge yourself for whatever your mind comes up with when you let it run wild. Daydreaming about Paris doesn't mean you need to buy a plane ticket. It could just lead you to croissants for dinner.*

EXTRA CREDIT: Take your daydreams one step further and create a vision board of things you see in your daydreams.

Make Natural Household Cleaners

Save money and play scientist in your own loo-lab!

THE BASIC IDEA: Make all kinds of different natural cleaners using ingredients you probably have around the house.

THE WHAT: You don't have to buy 14 different products to keep your place ship-shape! It's easy & fun to whip up all sorts of cleaners, from produce wash to chrome polish. Add some nice essential oils to make 'em smell good!

THE WHY: Making your own cleaners is empowering. It frees you from wasteful plastic consumption and countless Target runs! Plus, homemade cleaners can be more effective than store-bought, while leaving out yucky chemicals. Bonus: you'll feel like a real chemist as you mix up your potions!

ALONE-TIME SCALE: About how long does this hobby take?

MAYBE LIKE 15 MINUTES? — AT LEAST THE LENGTH OF A MOVIE. OR THREE. — YOU COULD BE HERE FOREVER!

(Circled: middle of scale, AT LEAST THE LENGTH OF A MOVIE. OR THREE.)

COZY HOBBY FYI'S

Do I need special tools?
(X) Yes ( ) No ( ) It depends

How cheap is this hobby?
( ) Free! (X) Cheap ( ) Not cheap

Can I do this on the toilet?
( ) Yes ( ) Your call (X) At your own risk

Can I do this in a nice, warm bath?
( ) Yes ( ) Awkwardly, maybe? (X) A thousand times no

How many times will I have to leave the bathroom?
( ) Never ever ( ) Maybe once? (X) Ugh like 3 times

EXTRA CREDIT: Go hardcore: make your own laundry soap & floor polish!

POTTY *talk*

I've been singing Shakira songs in front of my bathroom mirror into my hairbrush forever. It's like a daily routine.

—TAYLOR SWIFT

Play Brain Games

While you're just sitting there, you may as well get smarter.

THE BASIC IDEA: Pull double duty while you doodie. Get smart while you fart. Give your mind some glee while you pee. Sorry for all this potty humor, but this *is* a book about hobbies you can do in the crapper.

THE WHAT: Keep a cute lil' basket of brain teasers in the bathroom. You can buy books full of crosswords, puzzles, mazes, sudoku, word searches, or riddles. You can download apps to your phone or print stuff off the internet. Bonus: you'll get smarter while eliminating waste! Now that's genius!

THE WHY: Smart people agree, a great way to keep your brain active and flexible is to make it figure out the answer to 34-Across (*another word for puzzle, 6 letters*). Plus, puzzles are a sort of mental workout/ massage in one, because they also help you de-stress and decompress!

ALONE-TIME SCALE: About how long does this hobby take?

MAYBE LIKE 15 MINUTES? — AT LEAST THE LENGTH OF A MOVIE. OR THREE. — YOU COULD BE HERE FOREVER!

COZY HOBBY FYI'S

Do I need special tools?
(X) Yes ◯ No ◯ It depends

How cheap is this hobby?
◯ Free! (X) Cheap ◯ Not cheap

Can I do this on the toilet?
(X) Yes ◯ Your call ◯ At your own risk

Can I do this in a nice, warm bath?
◯ Yes (X) Awkwardly, maybe? ◯ A thousand times no

How many times will I have to leave the bathroom?
(X) Never ever ◯ Maybe once? ◯ Ugh like 3 times

EXTRA CREDIT: Create your own word searches to passive-aggressively communicate with other people in your household! Example: Make a word search containing words related to cleaning the bathroom. (You can find free templates online to create customized puzzles and word searches.)

Whittle a Corncob Pipe!

Master the time-honored tradition of hobos and talking snowmen!

THE BASIC IDEA: You too can make a real, fully functioning pipe out of nothing more than an ear of corn and a twig!

THE WHAT: Corncob pipes are a DIY wonder, made from the humblest of materials. All you need is a corncob, a knife and/or boring tool, and a small branch or piece of bamboo! Oh, and patience. Once it's finished, fill the bowl with some naturally grown tobacco, and pretend you're a real old-timer, or Frosty.

THE WHY: Corncob pipes are the most DIY way imaginable to smoke. In fact, they're so natural and homemade, they make smoking seem almost . . . *wholesome*.

EXTRA CREDIT: Learn to play the washboard and smoke a corncob pipe!

ALONE-TIME SCALE: About how long does this hobby take?

MAYBE LIKE 15 MINUTES? — AT LEAST THE LENGTH OF A MOVIE. OR THREE. — YOU COULD BE HERE FOREVER!

COZY HOBBY FYI'S

Do I need special tools?

(X) Yes ◯ No ◯ It depends

How cheap is this hobby?

◯ Free! (X) Cheap ◯ Not cheap

Can I do this on the toilet?

◯ Yes ◯ Your call (X) At your own risk

Can I do this in a nice, warm bath?

◯ Yes ◯ Awkwardly, maybe? (X) A thousand times no

How many times will I have to leave the bathroom?

◯ Never ever ◯ Maybe onoo? (X) Ugh like 3 times

GREAT MOMENTS IN *(BATHROOM)* HISTORY!

DID YOU KNOW?

The bathroom is an incredibly creative space. In a 2014 study, 72 percent of respondents said they came up with new ideas in the shower. In 1982, NASA engineer Lonnie Johnson invented the Super Soaker® in his bathroom. Ancient Greek scientist Archimedes discovered the "Archimedes Principle" while getting in a bath—a mathematical tool for measuring volume that is used to this day!

Spa Day!

YOU. DESERVE. IT.

THE BASIC IDEA: Pamper yourself like you're at a day spa with a fancy aesthetician. Except do it yourself in your very own bathroom, for free!

THE WHAT: Put that overhead lighting to good use and spend some time self-pampering yourself. Hop up on your counter and soak your toes while you polish your fingertips. Dry brush and put on a moisturizing face mask, then slip into a relaxing herbal bath.

THE WHY: Adding extra pampering to your life will not only make you shinier, but you'll smell better, too. Plus, you are worth it.

HOT TIP: *If you're scrimping, you can get decent face masks and other beauty stuff at the dollar store. You can also make them from ingredients in your kitchen (just google it)!*

ALONE-TIME SCALE: About how long does this hobby take?

MAYBE LIKE 15 MINUTES? — AT LEAST THE LENGTH OF A MOVIE. OR THREE. — YOU COULD BE HERE FOREVER!

COZY HOBBY FYI'S

Do I need special tools?
(X) Yes ( ) No ( ) It depends

How cheap is this hobby?
( ) Free! ( ) Cheap (X) Not cheap

Can I do this on the toilet?
( ) Yes (X) Your call ( ) At your own risk

Can I do this in a nice, warm bath?
(X) Yes ( ) Awkwardly, maybe? ( ) A thousand times no

How many times will I have to leave the bathroom?
(X) Never ever ( ) Maybe once? ( ) Ugh like 3 times

EXTRA CREDIT: Transform your bathroom into a serene-feeling home spa with rolled-up washcloths, candles, and the right playlist. You can even make your own cucumber water. Don't you deserve cucumber water? YES, YOU DESERVE CUCUMBER WATER.

Shadow Puppets

Pick up an entertaining skill you can take wherever you go!

THE BASIC IDEA: Learn to make silhouettes of all sorts of animals and fanciful creatures using your hands and a blank wall!

THE WHAT: You probably played shadow puppets a bit as a kid. Maybe you were lucky enough to have an adult around who knew how. Now YOU can be that magical grown-up who seems to create life using nothing more than her hands, a wall, and a light!

THE WHY: With just a bit of practice, you can create intriguing, adorable characters . . . for free, with no screen technology required. Shadow puppetry has been around for thousands of years, and may be the oldest form of "animation" known to humanity!

EXTRA CREDIT: Use cardboard and sticks to create sets, props, or other characters, and make a puppet show!

ALONE-TIME SCALE: About how long does this hobby take?

MAYBE LIKE 15 MINUTES? — AT LEAST THE LENGTH OF A MOVIE. OR THREE. — YOU COULD BE HERE FOREVER!

(Circled: 1 of 10 — MAYBE LIKE 15 MINUTES?)

COZY HOBBY FYI'S

Do I need special tools?

◯ Yes (X) No ◯ It depends

How cheap is this hobby?

(X) Free! ◯ Cheap ◯ Not cheap

Can I do this on the toilet?

(X) Yes ◯ Your call ◯ At your own risk

Can I do this in a nice, warm bath?

◯ Yes (X) Awkwardly, maybe? ◯ A thousand times no

How many times will I have to leave the bathroom?

(X) Never ever ◯ Maybe once? ◯ Ugh like 3 times

Mindfulness & Meditation

Ommmm. May a peaceful force be with you. Ommmm.

THE BASIC IDEA: Nurture your mind, body, and spirit with a simple at-home meditation practice. (You don't have to call it a practice, but it might make you feel more like a fancy meditation person.)

THE WHAT: Take a few quiet moments when you can be alone, undisturbed. Light a candle. Close your eyes. Breathe deeply into your belly for a count of three. Hold it for four. Exhale for five. Repeat. The goal here is to quiet your mind and find a little peace, if only for a minute.

THE WHY: Chances are, your bathroom is one of the few places where you can truly be alone. Fortunately, that kind of environment is ideal for mental health! Taking time to meditate or re-center yourself has countless benefits, including reduced stress, improved mood and focus, and even better health.

ALONE-TIME SCALE: About how long does this hobby take?

MAYBE LIKE 15 MINUTES? — AT LEAST THE LENGTH OF A MOVIE. OR THREE. — YOU COULD BE HERE FOREVER!

COZY HOBBY FYI'S

Do I need special tools?
◯ Yes ⊗ No ◯ It depends

How cheap is this hobby?
⊗ Free! ◯ Cheap ◯ Not cheap

Can I do this on the toilet?
⊗ Yes ◯ Your call ◯ At your own risk

Can I do this in a nice, warm bath?
⊗ Yes ◯ Awkwardly, maybe? ◯ A thousand times no

How many times will I have to leave the bathroom?
⊗ Never ever ◯ Maybe once? ◯ Ugh like 3 times

HOT TIP: *If you find yourself resisting meditation or never finding the right time or moment, simply close your eyes and count your breaths for five inhale/exhales. Do it in the shower or on the toilet. Then do it again the next morning.*

EXTRA CREDIT: As your mindfulness and meditation skills grow, stretch yourself to keep at it longer and longer. This is a muscle you're building, so go easy on yourself. Simply trying to stay in a meditative state for 15 seconds is a start!

You've got to go big when you're in the shower. There's no half-singing in the shower. You're either a rock star or an opera diva.

—JOSH GROBAN

Bonsai!

Create adorable fairy-sized live trees!

THE BASIC IDEA: Bonsai (pronounced "bone-sigh") is the Japanese & East Asian art of pruning trees and plants to look like perfectly proportioned mini-trees.

THE WHAT: Bonsai is part horticulture, part artistry, part meditation. It's also an ideal bathroom hobby, because it involves the pruning of roots as well as branches, and can get pretty messy! Plus, as everyone knows, gnomes and tree sprites are much more likely to appear if you're working in a nice, quiet place.

THE WHY: As mentioned, bonsai is more than simply cutting plants. It's got everything you need for a first-rate mindfulness and meditation practice . . . but also leaves you with something to show for it!

EXTRA CREDIT: Watch *The Karate Kid I & II* for extra inspo!

ALONE-TIME SCALE: About how long does this hobby take?

MAYBE LIKE 15 MINUTES? — AT LEAST THE LENGTH OF A MOVIE. OR THREE. — YOU COULD BE HERE FOREVER! (circled)

COZY HOBBY FYI'S

Do I need special tools?

(X) Yes ( ) No ( ) It depends

How cheap is this hobby?

( ) Free! ( ) Cheap (X) Not cheap

Can I do this on the toilet?

( ) Yes ( ) Your call (X) At your own risk

Can I do this in a nice, warm bath?

( ) Yes ( ) Awkwardly, maybe? (X) A thousand times no

How many times will I have to leave the bathroom?

( ) Never ever ( ) Maybe once? (X) Ugh like 3 times

Watch Other People Take Walks Online

Have an adventure in a foreign country without leaving your water closet!

THE BASIC IDEA: It's like taking a walk yourself, but you don't actually have to wear sneakers or look at a map!

THE WHAT: Loads of generous, adventurous, tech-y talented people record themselves taking walks in interesting places, and then upload them online. You can find a good walk in almost any city or town across the globe, just with one little internet search.

THE WHY: Maybe you can't take a trip right now or you've always been curious about that tiny town in Germany your mom is from. Or perhaps you wonder if

ALONE-TIME SCALE: About how long does this hobby take?

MAYBE LIKE 15 MINUTES? — AT LEAST THE LENGTH OF A MOVIE. OR THREE. — YOU COULD BE HERE FOREVER!

COZY HOBBY FYI'S

Do I need special tools?
(X) Yes ( ) No ( ) It depends

How cheap is this hobby?
( ) Free! ( ) Cheap (X) Not cheap

Can I do this on the toilet?
( ) Yes (X) Your call ( ) At your own risk

Can I do this in a nice, warm bath?
( ) Yes ( ) Awkwardly, maybe? (X) A thousand times no

How many times will I have to leave the bathroom?
( ) Never ever ( ) Maybe once? (X) Ugh like 3 times

snow falling in Paris is as romantic as it sounds? Now you can find out, right from your own toilet!

EXTRA CREDIT: If you actually do want to get some exercise, look into buying one of those bike pedal things that people use under their desks. You can attempt to move your feet while watching someone else do most of the huffing and puffing.

Learn about the Stars & Stuff

Learn to identify celestial dippers & bears—from the bathroom!

THE BASIC IDEA: Get to know your astral neighborhood—the sky where you live!

THE WHAT: You don't have to take a class to learn the names of stars, planets, and constellations—you don't even have to get off the can. With the right app, all you have to do is aim your phone at the sky to find all the nearby celestial bodies, day or night.

THE WHY: The sky is more entertaining than all the streaming platforms combined (and that's a lot!). Plus, you can navigate your ship when you become an old-timey sea captain!

HOT TIP: *Stargazing binoculars are easier than telescopes and will also work for bird-watching!*

ALONE-TIME SCALE: About how long does this hobby take?

MAYBE LIKE 15 MINUTES? — AT LEAST THE LENGTH OF A MOVIE. OR THREE. — YOU COULD BE HERE FOREVER!

COZY HOBBY FYI'S

Do I need special tools?

(X) Yes ( ) No ( ) It depends

How cheap is this hobby?

( ) Free! (X) Cheap ( ) Not cheap

Can I do this on the toilet?

( ) Yes (X) Your call ( ) At your own risk

Can I do this in a nice, warm bath?

( ) Yes ( ) Awkwardly, maybe? (X) A thousand times no

How many times will I have to leave the bathroom?

(X) Never ever ( ) Maybe once? ( ) Ugh like 3 times

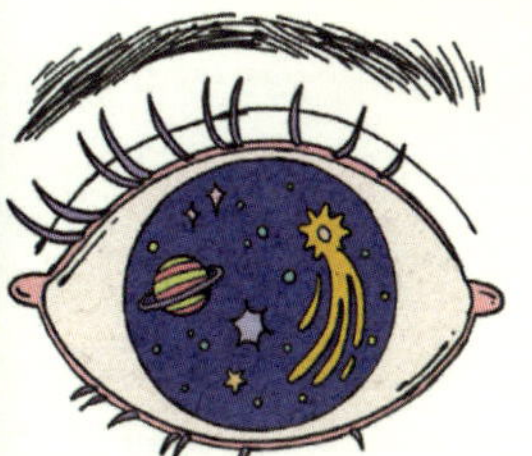

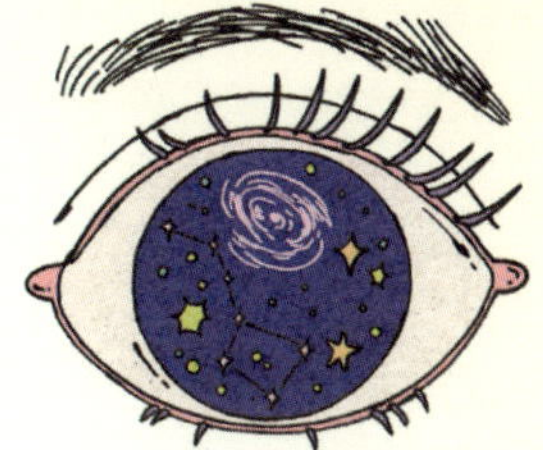

POTTY talk
You can change the world with a hot bath, if you sink into it from a place of knowing that you are worth profound care, even when you're dirty and rattled.
—ANNE LAMOTT

Make Pottery in the Powder Room

Explore your inner clay artist!

THE BASIC IDEA: Make ornaments, candle holders, tiny vases for dried flowers, or anything else you can dream of sculpting . . . in the bathroom!

THE WHAT: Imagine yourself all cozed up and crafting away in the comfort of your home pottery studio (AKA your bathroom!). You can do this—without a pottery wheel or paying class fees.

THE WHY: You can make gifts galore while expressing yourself creatively without leaving the sanctuary of your restroom. Plus, people will be impressed. Even clay creations that look like they were made by a toddler with a 10-cup-a-day coffee habit are impressive to people who've never worked with clay.

ALONE-TIME SCALE: About how long does this hobby take?

MAYBE LIKE 15 MINUTES? | AT LEAST THE LENGTH OF A MOVIE. OR THREE. | YOU COULD BE HERE FOREVER!

COZY HOBBY FYI'S

Do I need special tools?
○ Yes ⊗ No ○ It depends

How cheap is this hobby?
○ Free! ○ Cheap ⊗ Not cheap

Can I do this on the toilet?
○ Yes ○ Your call ⊗ At your own risk

Can I do this in a nice, warm bath?
○ Yes ○ Awkwardly, maybe? ⊗ A thousand times no

How many times will I have to leave the bathroom?
○ Never ever ⊗ Maybe once? ○ Ugh like 3 times

HOT TIP: *Air-dry clay is a miracle substance. It's easy to work with, a lot less messy than traditional clay, and just as much fun. It's also relatively cheap. Best of all: no kilns required!*

EXTRA CREDIT: After your creations are dry, you can also try glazing them! There are loads of colorful glazes available for air-dry clay and you can set up a little painting studio in the ol' john.

Pet Grooming

Your pet is gonna need a bath one of these days!

THE BASIC IDEA: Learn to groom your pet like a pro, without the cost (and humiliating hair bows).

THE WHAT: Lure Fluffy into a comfy state in the throne room, then BAM: brush her fur! BOOM: trim her nails! It's part hang time, part chore!

THE WHY: Taking care of your pet's beauty needs is much cheaper when you tend to them yourself! And since it has to get done, why not do it in your bathroom? Plus, if your fur baby tends to get freaked out by groomers, this will be a thousand times less traumatic for you both.

HOT TIP: *Keep a tub of treats, brushes, and pet clippers under the bathroom sink for easy, anytime access.*

EXTRA CREDIT: Decorate their collars or better yet, try to brush their teeth.

ALONE-TIME SCALE: About how long does this hobby take?

MAYBE LIKE 15 MINUTES? — AT LEAST THE LENGTH OF A MOVIE. OR THREE. — YOU COULD BE HERE FOREVER!

COZY HOBBY FYI'S

Do I need special tools?
(X) Yes ( ) No ( ) It depends

How cheap is this hobby?
( ) Free! (X) Cheap ( ) Not cheap

Can I do this on the toilet?
(X) Yes ( ) Your call ( ) At your own risk

Can I do this in a nice, warm bath?
( ) Yes ( ) Awkwardly, maybe? (X) A thousand times no

How many times will I have to leave the bathroom?
( ) Never ever ( ) Maybe once? (X) Ugh like 3 times

Declutter Your Phone

You're wasting time on it anyway. Why not waste time productively?

THE BASIC IDEA: In case no one has told you lately, your phone is a big, jumbled mess. Give that baby a (digital) cleanup!

THE WHAT: Do you really need 8K photos of your cat? Chances are no. Numerous apps and even built-in features on your phone can help you delete large files, dump old apps & organize your screens!

THE WHY: More available space on your phone means longer battery life, which is good news if you left your charger in another room and don't want to re-enter the world outside your comfort station. But also, everything holds energy, and you don't need to be carrying around oodles of screenshots and photos of people you don't know anymore. And you weren't using all those budgeting apps anyway, were you?

ALONE-TIME SCALE: About how long does this hobby take?

MAYBE LIKE 15 MINUTES? — AT LEAST THE LENGTH OF A MOVIE. OR THREE. — YOU COULD BE HERE FOREVER!

COZY HOBBY FYI'S

Do I need special tools?
◯ Yes ◯ No ⊗ It depends

How cheap is this hobby?
◯ Free! ⊗ Cheap ◯ Not cheap

Can I do this on the toilet?
⊗ Yes ◯ Your call ◯ At your own risk

Can I do this in a nice, warm bath?
◯ Yes ◯ Awkwardly, maybe? ⊗ A thousand times no

How many times will I have to leave the bathroom?
⊗ Never ever ◯ Maybe once? ◯ Ugh like 3 times

EXTRA CREDIT: Delete old texts. Delete old numbers you no longer need. Super mega bonus points: Go ahead and block that jerk, while you're at it. You know the one.

GREAT MOMENTS IN *(BATHROOM)* HISTORY!

DID YOU KNOW?

Kate Winslet and Susan Sarandon keep their Oscars in the bathroom. Singer Adele does the same with her Grammys. "In England, it's a tradition to put your plaques and photographs and awards and gold records and stuff in your bathroom," she explains. "I kick myself every day when I go for a poo and see my awards and think, 'Wow, I did good!'"

THE BIG CHEESE
BEST PAPER PLANE

Learn How to Sharpen Stuff

Once you go sharp, you'll never want to be dull again!

THE BASIC IDEA: Give your knives and scissors a whole new life and make 'em feel brand-new!

THE WHAT: Use a honing steel to straighten and flatten your blade, and then follow up with a sharpener or whetstone.

THE WHY: Sharpening a knife will make you look and feel like a total baddie. And though it seems counterintuitive, sharpened knives are actually much easier to use, require less pressure and effort, and are much safer than dull knives! Plus, you'll save money because you won't have to keep buying new knives every couple years.

ALONE-TIME SCALE: About how long does this hobby take?

MAYBE LIKE 15 MINUTES? | AT LEAST THE LENGTH OF A MOVIE. OR THREE. | YOU COULD BE HERE FOREVER!

COZY HOBBY FYI'S

Do I need special tools?
(X) Yes ( ) No ( ) It depends

How cheap is this hobby?
( ) Free! (X) Cheap ( ) Not cheap

Can I do this on the toilet?
( ) Yes ( ) Your call (X) At your own risk

Can I do this in a nice, warm bath?
( ) Yes ( ) Awkwardly, maybe? (X) A thousand times no

How many times will I have to leave the bathroom?
( ) Never ever (X) Maybe once? ( ) Ugh like 3 times

HOT TIP: *You can keep your knives sharp much longer by honing them on an old leather belt after sharpening them. (Check out how-to videos for proper technique!)*

EXTRA CREDIT: Learn to sharpen your yard clippers, mower blades, and scissors!

Crystal Magic!

Tap into the majesty of rock!

THE BASIC IDEA: Embrace these glorious minerals for fun, self-care, and magic.

THE WHAT: Crystals are solid minerals forged in the earth over millions of years, believed to possess amazing powers (kind of like superheroes . . . but rocks). Hold them, meditate with them, tell them your troubles. They won't judge. They've seen it all. They're literally like 12 million years old.

THE WHY: Hold a quartz in your hand. It's cool to the touch (and somehow calming), right? Told ya crystals were cool! Whether you're a science nerd, witch, or just a fan of pretty rocks, crystals are endlessly fascinating.

HOT TIP: *Check out a book or online guide to learn which crystals are believed to possess the powers you're looking for! Calming? Clarity? Confidence? Sex appeal? There's a crystal for your every mood!*

ALONE-TIME SCALE: About how long does this hobby take?

MAYBE LIKE 15 MINUTES? — AT LEAST THE LENGTH OF A MOVIE. OR THREE. — YOU COULD BE HERE FOREVER!

(8 of 10 circled)

COZY HOBBY FYI'S

Do I need special tools?
(X) Yes ( ) No ( ) It depends

How cheap is this hobby?
( ) Free! ( ) Cheap (X) Not cheap

Can I do this on the toilet?
( ) Yes ( ) Your call (X) At your own risk

Can I do this in a nice, warm bath?
(X) Yes ( ) Awkwardly, maybe? ( ) A thousand times no

How many times will I have to leave the bathroom?
(X) Never ever ( ) Maybe once? ( ) Ugh like 3 times

POTTY *talk*

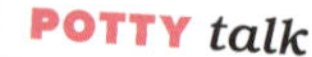

Always go to the bathroom when you have a chance.

—KING GEORGE V
of the UNITED KINGDOM

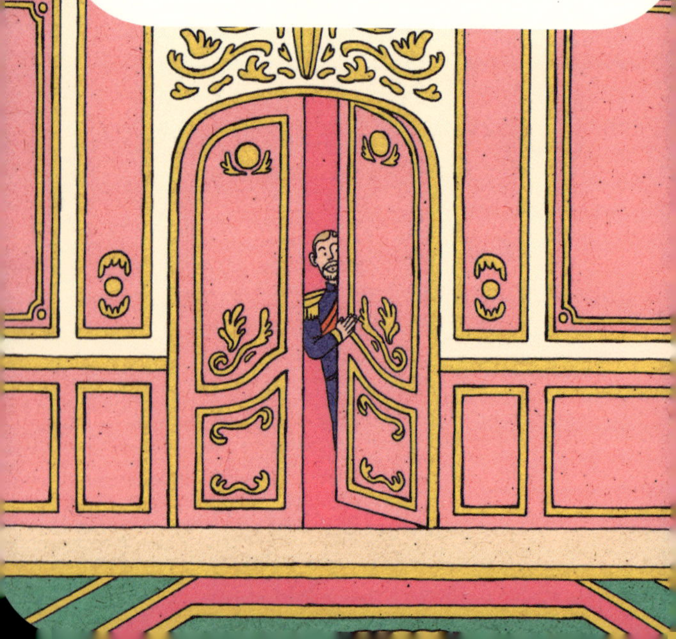

Now go
to the bathroom!